re
set

20 WAYS TO A CONSISTENT PRAYER LIFE

BOB SORGE

OASIS HOUSE · KANSAS CITY, MO

RESET: 20 Ways to a Consistent Prayer Life
Copyright © 2018 by Bob Sorge
Published by Oasis House
PO Box 522
Grandview, MO 64030-0522
816-767-8880

Editor: Edie Mourey
Cover designer: Andrew Beauman
Typesetter: Dale Jimmo

Special thanks to Andres Spyker for birthing the idea of this book, and to Tracey Sliker for landing the title.

ISBN: 978-1-937725-42-6
Library of Congress Control Number: 2017908679

For information on all Bob's books, go to www.oasishouse.com.

www.oasishouse.com
twitter.com/BOBSORGE
facebook.com/BobSorgeMinistry
Blog: bobsorge.com

To see Bob's films, go to youtube.com and enter a search for "Bob Sorge Channel"

Bob Sorge writes with inspiring insight and practical application. What I appreciate about this book is that it provides virtually anyone with the practical steps to get started in prayer. In these days, the Lord is highlighting the centrality of prayer in a believer's life. I encourage you, therefore, to accept the 20/20 challenge of this book, hit *Reset*, and just go!

Mike Bickle
International House of Prayer of Kansas City

Bob Sorge has spent his ministry life equipping believers for deeper intimacy with God. More than a prayer guide, this book is a peek into Bob's personal journey of pursuing the Father. If you want a more consistent prayer life and don't know where to start, this is the perfect book for you!

Robert Morris
Founding Pastor, Gateway Church, Dallas, TX
Bestselling author of *The Blessed Life, The God I Never Knew, Truly Free,* and *Frequency.*

I'm thrilled at *Reset*. The world needs a mighty prayer revival to bring us through the dark times we face. Bob concisely teaches us how to establish a prayer habit. I've had one for 35 years, and this book is an *amazing* beginning to yours.

Larry Stockstill
Pastor Emeritus, Bethany Church, Baton Rouge, LA

This book will take you on a devotional experience led by the Teacher Himself, Holy Spirit. As you walk with Him through these pages, allow Him to take you into new places of intimacy and communion with your Father. It's a journey worth taking.

Karen Wheaton, The RAMP, Hamilton, AL

What you read from our dear friend and brother, Bob Sorge, infuses you with life because he writes profoundly from the fires of suffering. Here you will excavate the foundations of prayer that will affect the history of both you and your world.

Lou Engle, President and Co-Founder of The Call

I read this while I rocked my infant girl, and I found, within the pages, that prayer resets are available even for moms of six (like me). Though my life hasn't gotten any less full in the last 20 days, my insides are alive in a new way because of the invitation of God within this book.

Sara Hagerty, author of *Every Bitter Thing is Sweet* and *Unseen: The Gift of Being Hidden in a World that Loves to be Noticed*

Everyone values the importance of prayer, and we all want to pray in a significant way. But for many of us the way seems confusing and intimidating. Bob simply makes the goal attainable. Want a fresh start? Do yourself a favor and read this gem!

Andres Spyker, Pastor, Mas Vida, Mexico

RESET

20 Ways to a Consistent Prayer Life

INSTRUCTIONS

Buckle up, you're on the threshold of a spiritual adventure. This handbook will guide your quest to grow a meaningful, intimate relationship with Jesus Christ.

Here's a few suggestions to maximize your 20-day journey:

✦ Bring your Bible, notepad, and pen each day to your Reset.

✦ Most chapters invite you to write out a Scripture or make some kind of notation. If you're reading this book in an electronic format, therefore, I suggest you use a paper notepad alongside your device.

✦ ⏻ This icon invites you to pause and reflect on what you've just read.

✦ At the back of this book you'll find some optional questions for group discussion. When possible, do your Reset with a small group.

✦ For those on social media, you can post a pic to your friends and say, I'm on a #PrayerReset.

✦ Visit PrayerReset.com for a video introduction to this guide.

Have you been frustrated over previous attempts at daily devotions? Hit Reset. God is with you. You're about to discover new realms of joy in His presence!

Day 1
DESIRE

A meaningful and consistent prayer life—that's what you want. That's why you're here. You know prayer has the potential to be delightful, reciprocal, whole-hearted, invigorating, and powerful. And you want it.

It all starts with burning desire for Christ.

Picture it for a moment. You're holed up in a quiet nook; the door is closed; the chair is comfortable; you've got a mug, and your Bible is open; it's your favorite time of day. And now you start doing your favorite thing—talking to your best Friend, Jesus.

It's simple talk, really. Everyday language. You express your adoration, thanks, and devotion. No topic is off limits. And there's no end to the things you admire in Him: His amazing salvation, majestic glory, winsome nature, and endless mercy. He's your dwelling place forever.

Incredibly, Jesus Himself sits with us and assures us of His presence. As we're under the blood of Christ, the Father's acceptance wows us. We're washed and renewed by the word and the Spirit. Love is awakened as we meditate in Scripture. Our spirit is ignited, our body is made alive, and our soul is restored. We talk to Him and He talks to us in the language of intimate friendship.

Ahhh, it doesn't get any better than this! This is what we want!

> *One thing I have desired of the LORD, that will I seek: That I may dwell in the house of the LORD all the days of my life, to behold the beauty of the LORD, and to inquire in His temple. (Ps 27:4)*

In Psalm 27:4, David described his foremost desire. Make it yours, too. Use this verse to express the longings of your heart. **PRAY**.

- ✦ Tell Him there's only one thing you really want.
- ✦ Express your desire to seek Him diligently.
- ✦ Tell Him you want to live in His presence continually.
- ✦ Yearn to behold His beauty.
- ✦ Inquire into His will, thoughts, plans, and wisdom.

Take a few minutes to express these things to God. ⏻

See how inspired the disciples were when they watched Jesus pray.

> *Now it came to pass, as He was praying in a certain place, when He ceased, that one of His disciples said to Him, "Lord, teach us to pray, as John also taught his disciples." So He said to them, "When you pray, say: Our Father in heaven, hallowed be Your name." (Luke 11:1-2)*

Jesus' prayer life inspired them, so they asked to be taught to pray the same way. He was quick to respond. The way Jesus taught about prayer showed how important it was to Him.

PRAY. Think about how real and engaged Jesus' prayer life must have been. Repeat the disciples' request: *Lord, teach me to pray. Like You prayed.* ⏻

Grab a pen. What's your dream prayer life? Ask Him to help you express in writing what you want your prayer life to be. Articulate what you hope will happen in the next 20 days.

I'm doing this Reset because I'm after a prayer life that is _____

_____

_____

David's "one thing" desire was also Paul's "one thing." We see it in this passage:

> *That I may know Him....But one thing I do... (Phil 3:10, 13)*

Paul's all-consuming desire was to know Christ. That's why he prayed, and that's why we pray. There's one thing above all else that we crave—to know Jesus more.

PRAY.

✦ Tell Him how deeply you want an enduring prayer life.

✦ *Jesus, I want to know You.*

✦ Confess that you're too weak in your own strength to go the distance. *Without You I can do nothing, Lord Jesus.*

✦ Express your complete dependence on His strength.

✦ Call on His grace for help!

✦ Ask for holy desire to burn ever brighter in your heart.

✦ Receive grace to run your race.

The first foundation stone in a prayer life is desire. By His grace, Jesus is giving you a burning desire to pray. Have a great day!

🖉 **NOTES**

Day 2
DECIDE

Reminder: Yesterday we identified our longing for "one thing": to know Christ. May this fiery desire for a friendship with Jesus continue to burn and grow all our days!

Our human will is one of our most valuable possessions. God gave us the power of decision. Our decisions determine the course of our life and destiny.

Think of how the course of your life has been directed by decisions you've made: Faith. College. Career. Marriage. Kids. Church. Friendships. A simple decision can change everything.

In the same way, every holy resolve to obey God changes our lives profoundly.

A consistent prayer life starts with a calculated, heroic decision. Your decision today to pray could determine the course of your destiny.

A resolve to pray is crucial, but willpower alone isn't enough. To cultivate a prayer life requires both our resolve and God's help. We need His grace to follow through on this decision. Paul pointed to this in the following passage.

> *Work out your own salvation with fear and trembling; for it is God who works in you both to will and to do for His good pleasure. (Phil 2:12-13)*

A prayer reset requires work from both us and God. While we're working it out, God is working it in. Our resolve combined with His grace produces concrete change.

A life-altering choice is before you. Decide, by God's grace, to cultivate a prayer life.

You're not experimenting or giving it a try. You're going all in. You're burning the bridges and abandoning your heart to God because you know He's going to help you. Your decision is firm. ⏻

I recommend a paper Bible during this Reset, but if an electronic version helps you more, that's great too. While this book uses the New King James Version, choose the version that helps you most. Now open your Bible to Psalm 20.

Slowly read each verse in Psalm 20 and quietly tell the Lord what you're thinking as you read each verse. Then, write either verse 4 here or the verse that grabs your attention most.

PRAY. Take a couple minutes to ponder that verse and what it means to your life. Talk to the Lord about it. ⏻

Throughout this Reset we will have a daily reading in Psalms, the Gospels, and the Epistles because I'd like to win you over to this practice for life. We've done one of Paul's epistles and a psalm so far today, so now let's do a Gospel reading. Look at these words of Jesus.

> "But one thing is needed, and Mary has chosen that good part, which will not be taken away from her." (Luke 10:42)

What did Mary choose? She decided to sit at Jesus' feet and hear His words. She wasn't dissuaded by the pressure she felt to help prepare dinner for everyone. Listening to Jesus was an opportunity she wasn't about to miss.

Jesus said just *one thing is needed*—hearing and retaining His word. When we decide to sit before Him, read His word and talk to Him, we're agreeing with Him that this is the most necessary thing.

PRAY. Ask the Lord to give you insight into the Scriptures, over the next 20 days, that nothing can take away from you. ⏻

Have you decided to devote yourself in a fresh way to God? If so, you're invited to sign the following statement.

My 20-Day Promise to God

I hereby resolve, by God's grace, to spend at least 20 minutes a day in the secret place with Jesus, for the next 20 days.

Signature _____

Date _____

PRAY. Say *yes* to Jesus' call. Express your desires and intentions. Stay right here until your 20 minutes are up. Ask for help to follow Him as a true disciple. You may even want to post your resolve to your friends using #PrayerReset.

May your entire day be characterized by holy resolve!

✎ NOTES

Day 3
REACH

Even though your decision is firm, it's probably being challenged already. Have you been hit with distractions, temptations, or discouragement? These are common to everyone's experience.

Our adversary focuses on our past failures. He doesn't want us praying, so he'll try to discourage us by reminding us of every failed prayer attempt in the past.

Have you felt apprehension, wondering if this Reset might sputter out? Then look at this verse:

But one thing I do, forgetting those things which are behind and REACHING FORWARD to those things which are ahead, I press toward the goal for the prize of the upward call of God in Christ Jesus. (Phil 3:13-14)

To cultivate a prayer life, *reach forward.* Look straight ahead, put your eyes on the goal of a habitual prayer life, say a prayer, and *reach*—with all your heart.

Push the delete button on every past failure. Has your quiet time lost momentum in the past? Hit delete. Have you lacked discipline and resolve? Hit delete. Has something persistently hindered you? Hit delete. Determine to forget the things—both positive and negative—that are behind you. By God's grace, delete it all.

Hit Reset, and *reach forward* with all your soul. Jesus is helping you to see the kind of prayer life He has for you. He's enabling you to see it because He knows you won't reach for something you can't see.

PRAY. Take a couple minutes and pray from Philippians 3:13-14 (above). Ask your heavenly Father, in Jesus' name, to help you forget the past and press forward toward the goal of a consistent prayer life. ⏻

Asking for mercy is a powerful prayer. What is mercy? It's the kindness of God to get us going in the right direction—in spite of ourselves. As you reach forward for new momentum in prayer, the mercy of God surrounds and empowers you. Mercy means this time is new!

As you reach for mercy, ponder these verses:

> *If I say, "My foot slips," Your mercy, O LORD, will hold me up. Ps 94:18)*
>
> *The LORD takes pleasure in those who fear Him, in those who hope in His mercy. (Ps 147:11)*

PRAY. Take a few minutes to talk to the Lord about these two verses. If you've lost your footing in the past, call out for mercy. Tell Him how much you rely on His help.

Now, thank Him for enabling you to reach for a prayer life that will endure all your days. ⏻

Look at this invitation from our Lord Jesus.

> *"If anyone desires to come after Me, let him deny himself, and take up his cross daily, and follow Me." (Luke 9:23)*

You're not simply reaching for a new prayer habit, you're reaching for Jesus. You want to see Him, know Him, be close to Him, lay hold of Him. The cross of Jesus has awakened you, and now you're longing to be filled with His love.

PRAY. Say yes to His call. Tell Him how eagerly you want to come after Him. Talk to Him about Luke 9:23 until your 20 minutes are up.

Heavenly Father, thank You for giving me a new start in prayer. I turn my back on all my past failures and reach forward for Your high calling. Increase my desire to pray. Jesus, I'm following You and never looking back. Only forward. Amen.

Have a great day as you hit *delete* on all that's behind and *reach* for more of Him!

✏ NOTES

Day 4
FIGHT

Reminder: : Yesterday we placed behind us every failed attempt to pray and decided to *reach* for the prayer life God is calling us to. One more time, with all your heart, reach forward.

Distractions. They're probably the most universal hindrance to prayer. When we decide to pray, it seems like everything in creation collaborates to pull our attention in other directions.

You're in a war for your prayer life. I urge you, therefore, to *demonize distractions*. Decide right now that anything seeking to draw your attention away from prayer is your enemy. Declare war. Mobilize an offensive against every distraction.

On Day 1, we quoted Psalm 27:4 where David said he desired to seek just one thing—to dwell in the Lord's presence all his days. But I want to point out that the verses that precede and follow it mention warfare. Here's the verses that follow Psalm 27:4.

> *For in the time of trouble He shall hide me in His pavilion; in the secret place of His tabernacle He shall hide me; He shall set me high upon a rock. And now my head shall be lifted up above my enemies all around me. (Psa 24:5-6)*

Warfare surrounds prayer because the place of prayer will always be contested. *You have an enemy who doesn't want you praying.*

PRAY. Ask God for a warring, militant spirit—for mettle in your soul. Receive grace to resist and overcome anything that hinders your prayer life.

This is war. Ask for strength to fight. ⏻

Okay, let's go after this thing. When Paul spoke of the believer's warfare in Ephesians 6, he urged us to put on the whole armor of God so we can stand against the wiles of the devil. He told us to clothe ourselves with truth, righteousness, the preparation of the gospel of peace, and the shield of faith. Then he closed the passage with this exhortation:

> *And take the helmet of salvation, and the sword of the Spirit, which is the word of God; praying always with all prayer and supplication in the Spirit. (Eph 6:17-18)*

The purpose of getting clothed with the armor of God, according to Paul, is that we might *pray*. Prayer assumes there will be a fight. To overcome in prayer, we must first get dressed for the battle.

Jesus spoke of our fight with the devil in this manner:

> *"Those by the wayside are the ones who hear; then the devil comes and takes away the word out of their hearts, lest they should believe and be saved." (Luke 8:12)*

Jesus has called us to pray, but the devil tries to use distractions to steal our prayer life from us. And the cares of life try to choke it (see Luke 8:14).

What things distract you from praying? Maybe it's things like the computer, phone, chores, a busy schedule, social media, TV, etc. Take a moment and write down the main things that distract your prayer time.

1. _____   2. _____

3. _____   4. _____

PRAY. Ask God for a specific strategy to combat these distractions.

Once God gives you the strategy, write it down below. Be real practical. ⏻

How I will fight each distraction, by God's grace:

1. _____

2. _____

3. _____

4. _____

Personally, one of my big distractions during prayer is that I often think of a new task I need to do. Then my head starts obsessing about that task. Here's how I've learned to war against that distraction: I take a notepad and pen to my secret place. When I think of a task I need to do, I write it down. Now I know I won't forget to do it. That assurance helps me push aside the distracting thoughts and return to prayer.

PRAY. Use the rest of your time to talk to the Lord about the distractions that derail you most. This is war! Ask the Holy Spirit to help you fight fiercely for a faithful prayer life.

By God's grace we overcome. Rejoice in the Lord!

✎ NOTES

_____

_____

_____

_____

Day 5
PLACE

Reminder: Yesterday was militant. We decided to take on everything that tries to divert our prayer focus. What are you doing right now to combat each distraction? Again, ask the Lord to help you win the war on distractions.

Today let's examine the *place* where you pray. Because it's very important to the success of your prayer Reset.

Jesus addressed the place of private prayer by painting a picture:

"But you, when you pray, go into your room, and when you have shut your door, pray to your Father who is in the secret place; and your Father who sees in secret will reward you openly." (Matt 6:6)

Jesus' advice? Build your prayer life upon the bed-rock of a secluded location. Find a room where you can withdraw from others, close the door, and have personal time with your Father.

Jesus gave a guaranteed way to get in the Father's presence. He said the Father *is in the secret place,* and when we shut our door we are immediately with Him. Instant intimacy. All you have to do, to meet with the Father, is shut your door.

In Jesus' case, He didn't have a room where He could isolate Himself from others, so He went out-doors *to a solitary place* for prayer (Mark 1:35). That's the idea behind *shut your door.* Jesus meant we should find a place of solitude.

Psalm 91 speaks marvelously of this meeting place with God. Write out Psalm 91:1 here:

This abiding relationship with the Father starts by withdrawing to the secret place of prayer, but then it never stops as we maintain that same intimacy with Him throughout the day. He wants to reveal to us the secrets of how to live in His presence all day long.

PRAY. Ask God to show you where your secret place should be. If you can't think of a place right away, stay here until the Lord gives it to you. Is it a room in your home? Your car? Outdoors? ⏻

Write down the specific *place* where you are resolved to pray during this 20-day Reset.

My secret place of prayer is:

PRAY. Take a little time to ask for help to get to your place of solitude every day.

By the way, your car can be a great place to pray. But don't drive during your Reset. Park it and pray. Then, when you drive away, keep praying.

> *Pray without ceasing. (1 Thess. 5:17)*

That little verse is one of the most challenging of all Scripture. And it's also one of the most amazing, because it reveals the Lord has made possible an ongoing conversation with Him that is so meaningful it never stops. What happens during a 20-minute Reset doesn't stop when the 20 minutes are over; rather, it fires up something that continues throughout the remainder of our day.

That little verse is the great aspiration of every believer with a noble heart for all of God. What we're all aiming for is a prayer life that becomes an unceasing, vibrant, 24/7 reality.

Getting to your *place* of prayer every day is so

wise. It helps you make unceasing prayer the quest of your lifetime.

Lord Jesus, help me to follow You every day to my secret place. And may that which happens there color everything I do every day.

You're going to have a fantastic day today with Jesus!

 NOTES

Day 6
CLOCK

Reminder: Yesterday we landed on a place to pray for these 20 days. You're in that place right now. Tell the Lord you have obeyed His call to find a specific place for prayer, your door is shut, and you love being with Him here.

Today let's examine the *time of day* when we pray. When seeking to grow a new habit, consistency is a key ingredient. I recommend therefore, if at all possible, to pray at the same time each day during these 20 days. Labor to go to the same *place* at the same *time* each day. Or get as close as you possibly can. This will give your Reset the best chance to take root.

When the gospel writers spoke of the time of day Jesus typically prayed, it was often at night or in the morning.

Now in the morning, having risen a long while before daylight, He went out and departed to a solitary place; and there He prayed. (Mark 1:35)

Many who teach on prayer advocate praying first thing in the morning. That's a tangible way to place Jesus first in our day. When we tithe, we're placing Him first in our finances; with morning prayer we're placing Him first in our schedule.

Some folks are morning people. But not everyone. Therefore, I encourage you to schedule your prayer time not automatically for the *first* part of your day but strategically for the *best* part of your day. Let me explain.

Examine the rhythms of your body clock. Most of us have a certain time of day when we are most energetic, engaged, and creative. At what time of day are you at your *best*?

The time of day I'm most alert is:

PRAY. Consecrate your best time of day to the Lord. Like everything else in your life, tell Him it's His. ⏻

Psalm 63 gives the impression that David was a morning person.

> *O God, You are my God; early will I seek You; my soul thirsts for You; my flesh longs for You in a dry and thirsty land where there is no water. (Ps 63:1)*

David resolved to seek the Lord *early*. To seek the Lord *early* means three things to me: 1) I should seek

Him early in life, in my youthful years; 2) I should seek Him in the early stages of troubles and trials; and 3) I should seek Him early in the day.

PRAY. Take a couple minutes to pray from Psalm 63:1. Express to the Lord how thirsty you are for Him. *Early will I seek You.* ⏻

Here's today's reading in the epistles:

> *Therefore gird up the loins of your mind, be sober. (1 Pet 1:13)*

To *gird up the loins of your mind* probably meant to muster the best energies of your mind so you can pray and serve God effectively. Our best mental energies often surface around a certain time of day.

Write down (again) your best time of day: _____

Write what you are typically doing at that time of day:

Now comes the challenging part. What can you do to align your 20-minute prayer Reset with that time of day? How much spiritual violence might this require on your part? Ideally, you want to carve your prayer time into a distraction-free slot when you're at your best mentally.

PRAY. Ask the Lord how you can make this happen. What can you adjust in your schedule so that your secret place coincides with your best time of day? Even if it's not possible to do it at the same time every day, what's the most consistent option possible? Once He shows you the best time(s) of day your schedule will permit, nail down your resolution.

I resolve by God's grace to place my prayer time, during this 20-day reset, at the following time of day: (How close to the minute can you specify?)

The rigorous decision to pray at a certain time tomorrow is made tonight. Because what I do tonight determines what I can do tomorrow. To be alert in tomorrow's appointment with God, I must get to bed in good time tonight.

Ask the Lord for grace to wrestle down this 20-minute time window *every day.*

And be there—tomorrow!

✎ NOTES

Day 7
REPENT

When we meditate in Scripture, we set ourselves up to be challenged by the Spirit of truth. He convicts of sin so we might repent.

Jesus' first call to His generation was to repent (Mark 1:15), and it's still the first thing He calls us to.

Repentance. An earthquake on the inside. It's a regular and ongoing discipline for every disciple of Christ. Its basic idea is *change*. It says both *no* and *yes*. Repentance says *no* to the sinful behaviors He's showing us, and *yes* to the new actions and attitudes He's inviting us into.

A commitment to repentance realizes that as long as we're breathing we're in need of personal change.

Repentance is often a response to seeing more of God. For example, Jesus once told His disciples to launch into the lake and lower their nets for a catch of fish. They had caught nothing all night, but at the word of Christ they obeyed. Immediately, they caught so many fish their nets began to break. Peter's response was to repent.

> *When Simon Peter saw it, he fell down at Jesus' knees, saying, "Depart from me, for I am a sinful man, O Lord!" (Luke 5:8)*

When Peter witnessed Christ's glory, he realized how sinful he was. The same happens with us. When He reveals to us fresh glimpses of His magnificence, repentance is our natural response.

PRAY. Ask to see Him. Express the cry of your heart for greater revelation into the excellences of Christ. ⏻

A disciple hides no secrets from Christ. That Judas Iscariot hid his pilfering from Jesus demonstrated that he was no true disciple. True disciples open the doors of their soul wide to the Savior's search.

Look how David prayed:

> *Search me, O God, and know my heart. (Ps 139:23)*

David wanted the Lord to know every dark place in his heart. He knew he could never overcome that which remained hidden. When we acknowledge our sin, grace immediately empowers us to turn from it and toward Jesus in affectionate obedience.

PRAY. Take a few minutes to pray David's marvelous prayer, *Search me. Know me.* Resolve to never hide anything from your Savior. Express how eagerly you want repentance and change to always be your companions. Nothing is out of bounds to His searching gaze. ⏻

One element in repentance is the transformation of the mind:

> *And do not be conformed to this world, but be transformed by the renewing of your mind, that you may prove what is that good and acceptable and perfect will of God. (Rom 12:2)*

Our minds are renewed when we allow the truth of God's word to change how we think. The best change happens from the inside out, starting first in the heart and then demonstrating itself in action.

PRAY. Take a few minutes to meditate on Romans 12:2. Ask Him to open your understanding to the verse. *Lord, transform my mind so that I no longer think like the world. I want to think like You do. Give me Your good and perfect will.* ⏻

Is there anything the Holy Spirit has been nudging you to repent of recently? If so, write down in the space below what He is challenging you to change. Or write a recent change He has helped you make.

As you leave your place of prayer now, whisper a prayer along these lines: *Lord Jesus, as I meditate in Your word, I commit to turn away from anything that needs to go. Help me by Your grace to live a life of repentance. I love You.*

✎ NOTES

Day 8
CLEANSE

Reminder: Yesterday we resolved to live a life of repentance. We invited the gaze of Jesus to search every part of our heart. Say it again to Him, *Know me, Lord.*

After repentance comes cleansing. One way believers are cleansed is by what Scripture calls the sprinkling of the blood of Christ (Heb 12:24; 1 Pet 1:2). That is not customary language in our culture, so let me explain what the Bible means by it.

The idea of *sprinkling* comes from Old Testament times when the high priest would dip his fingers and sprinkle the blood of the sacrifice on various things, such as the altar, the priests, the people, and the mercy seat. That practice pointed to the cross of Jesus. Now, Jesus sprinkles and washes us with His own blood which He shed on Calvary (Rev 1:5).

Jesus' blood is the most powerful detergent in the

universe. It's the only thing that cleanses someone's conscience.

Here's the primary New Testament passage that speaks of being sprinkled by the blood of Jesus:

> *Having boldness to enter the Holiest by the blood of Jesus...let us draw near with a true heart in full assurance of faith, having our hearts sprinkled from an evil conscience. (Heb 10:19,22)*

Two things accuse us of sin: our conscience and Satan (the accuser). Where one leaves off, the other picks up. Both are completely silenced by the sprinkling of the blood of Christ. The blood of Christ washes our conscience so thoroughly that we actually *feel* clean. To feel clean before God is the best feeling in the world!

When Satan accuses us of sin, the blood of Jesus silences him. Revelation 12:10-11 says we overcome the accuser by the blood of the Lamb. When we're covered by the blood of Christ, the accuser is muzzled. The blood shuts him up. This is great news.

You don't have to get sprinkled with blood only once in your life—just as you don't have to shower just once in your life. You can get cleansed by Christ's blood as frequently as you get defiled in the world. For most of us, that's every day.

PRAY. I suggest this simple prayer, *Jesus, sprinkle me with Your blood.* By faith, see yourself under the blood of Christ. Now your conscience is cleansed. You're beyond condemnation or accusation.

David also prayed for cleansing:

> *Purge me with hyssop, and I shall be clean; wash me, and I shall be whiter than snow. (Ps 51:7)*

A branch of hyssop was used to place the blood of the Passover lamb on the doorposts of a house (Exod 12:22). Hyssop, therefore, represented the cleansing of the lamb's blood. David was confident that God's washing would leave him clean both inside and out.

PRAY. Express your confidence in the blood of Jesus. Give thanks to God for such a glorious provision. Worship the Lamb of God who is worthy of all honor and praise. Rejoice in how clean you are right now! ⏻

Take some advice from Jesus:

> *"Seek first the kingdom of God and His righteousness."* (Matt 6:33)

God's righteousness is given to us when we place our faith in the cross of Christ. Why did Jesus tell us to make righteousness our first pursuit? Because His righteousness makes us bold to draw near to the throne of grace. Jesus told us to seek His righteousness first because He wants us to draw near Him in intimacy.

Decide, therefore, to get cleansed every day by the blood of Christ and draw near to God. This is how we seek God's righteousness and honor the sacrifice of Calvary.

Stop for a minute. This is an important moment in your prayer Reset. You're putting down a marker in your history with God. You're resolving to get cleansed daily by the sprinkled blood of Christ. This means that every day the voice of your conscience will be satisfied and the accuser will be silenced. You'll have great boldness to draw near to God every day. ⏻

☐ *By checking this box, I indicate my holy resolve to get sprinkled with the blood of Christ every day.*

PRAY. Ask God to remind you every day to get cleansed spiritually. Tell Him you intend to seek His righteousness continually. Thank Him for making a way, through the cross, for you to live in His presence all day, every day.

You are super-clean right now in the presence of your Father. Enjoy your stay in the throne room today!

✎ NOTES

Day 9
THANKS

> **Reminder:** Cleanse your conscience today. *Jesus, sprinkle me with Your blood.* Rejoice that all accusation is silenced by the blood of Christ and draw near to Him with boldness.

In this prayer Reset, you're experiencing fresh grace to come into the Lord's presence every day. And He told us, in His word, how He prefers we approach Him. Here's the best way to draw near to God:

> *Enter into His gates with thanksgiving, and into His courts with praise. Be thankful to Him, and bless His name. (Ps 100:4)*

The Lord loves it when we come into His presence with thanksgiving and praise. Sometimes in our distress, we come to Him with the agonized cries of a broken heart, and He never despises that. But even in our times of greatest despondency, our first words can still be *thank You*.

When you step into His room, let it be with a word of thanks and praise. Are you so distressed that you can't think of anything to thank Him for?

When you first meet up with someone you haven't seen for a while, usually your greeting is gracious and welcoming. "It's great to see you again!" Your first words usually aren't, "We need to talk."

Same for God. He appreciates when the opener to the conversation is characterized by thanksgiving, praise, and blessing.

PRAY. Just do it. Act upon Psalm 100:4 (above). Express thanks for something specific, and bless His name. This is a perfect way to start your daily prayer time. ⏻

Praise His *name*. Every name of God expresses something wonderful about the nature of His character and attributes. Personally, language for praise comes more easily when I consider His greatness in four ways:

 ✔ I praise His name (Ps 7:17)

 ✔ I praise His word (Ps 56:4, 10)

 ✔ I praise His works (Ps 78:4)

 ✔ I praise His power (Ps 21:13)

PRAY. Take a minute with each one to offer thanks and praise. These four qualities of God's greatness provide a fabulous framework for daily praise. ⏻

Jesus offered thanks to His Father frequently. Here's one example:

> *Then they took away the stone from the place where the dead man was lying. And Jesus lifted up His eyes and said, "Father, I thank You that You have heard Me." (John 11:41)*

Before Jesus raised Lazarus from the dead in John 11, He gave thanks. He also gave thanks before breaking the loaves and fish, before instituting the Lord's Supper, and before meals. For Him, thanksgiving was a way to open the conversation.

In giving instructions concerning prayer, Paul also spoke of the centrality of thanksgiving.

> *Be anxious for nothing, but in everything by prayer and supplication, with thanksgiving, let your requests be made known to God. (Phil 4:6)*

Thanksgiving is added to prayer much like salt to food. You can eat food without salt, but salt makes the meal much more enjoyable. Similarly, God will receive us if we pray without offering thanksgiving, but thanksgiving makes the exchange more delightful to Him.

Salvation, forgiveness, acceptance, mercy, grace, lovingkindness—His word, His name, His works, His power—we have sooo much to be thankful for!

I'll confess my forgetfulness here. Although I *feel* thankful to God most of the time, many times I forget to actually *verbalize* it. Thanksgiving needs to be spoken. That's why this prompter is helpful for me. I need to be reminded to actually express my thanksgiving and praise at the start of my prayer time.

PRAY. Ask the Lord for a way to remember to include thanksgiving in each day's praise. Once He shows you a way of remembering, write your strategy down here.

_____

_____

_____

Lord Jesus, I'm asking You to make thanksgiving and praise an habitual part of my daily prayer life.

As you step into your day now, go with a happy heart of gratefulness for the multitude of His mercies!

✐ **NOTES**

_____

_____

_____

_____

_____

_____

Day 10
#PRAYREAD

Reminder: Come into His presence with thanksgiving and praise. After you receive the sprinkling of blood, offer thanksgiving. Praise His name, word, works, and power.

Let's talk about praying the Scriptures. That's what I'm meaning by #PrayRead. Praying the Scriptures is the central pillar in a life of prayer. It's the juice that jazzes our prayer life.

You may have noticed that we've been praying the Scriptures each day during this Reset. Let's drill down on this to maximize its potential.

Jesus modeled this kind of prayer during His crucifixion. Of His seven sayings on the cross, three were taken from Psalms. For example, during His crucifixion Jesus prayed from Psalm 22:1.

> *At the ninth hour Jesus cried out with a loud voice, saying, "Eloi, Eloi, lama sabachthani?" which is translated, "My God, My God, why have You forsaken Me?" (Mark 15:34)*

When you are praying Scripture, therefore, you are following the example of the Master. ⏻

View the Bible as providing language for prayer. Many verses are excellent springboards for conversation with God.

Some of the easiest passages to #PrayRead are the various prayers in the Bible. The apostles wrote many prayers in their letters, and they're excellent fodder for #PrayReading. For example, this prayer of Paul's is great to use:

> *For this reason we also, since the day we heard it, do not cease to pray for you, and to ask that you may be filled with the knowledge of His will in all wisdom and spiritual understanding; that you may walk worthy of the Lord, fully pleasing Him, being fruitful in every good work and increasing in the knowledge of God; strengthened with all might, according to His glorious power, for all patience and longsuffering with joy. (Col 1:9-11)*

PRAY. Let's use the rest of our time today to pray from this passage. First, ask God to work everything in those verses into your own heart and life. Make mention of specific situations in which you want His will.

Second, think of someone whom you would like

to bless in prayer today. Got a name? Now, begin to pray for that person according to each phrase above.

→ Lord, may _____ (name of person) be filled with the knowledge of Your will.

→ Help _____ to walk worthy of You. At work, at school, at play, every minute of every day.

→ May _____ please You fully in every word and deed.

→ Empower _____ to be productive in good works.

→ May _____ increase in the knowledge of God.

→ Fill _____ with Your mighty power to endure in faith with joy, even when life is painful.

If you're aware of certain needs in that person's life, mention them as you pray.

Once you've finished praying Colossians 1:9-11 for that person, would you like to offer the same prayer for others in your circle of friends? This is a powerful passage to pray for virtually everyone you know.

You could offer the prayer of this passage for your national president, political and civic leaders, and any other officials for whom you care. The Bible is chock full of marvelous verses to pray over your national leaders. When praying from Scripture, sometimes you're simply telling God what He tells you to tell Him.

As time allows, pray the six requests of Colossians 1:9-11 for some other people who are dear to you. ⏻

Another marvelous way to #PrayRead the Scriptures is during your daily Bible reading. While reading, be on alert for a phrase you'll be inspired to pray in the moment. As you do, your Bible reading times will morph into a delightful conversation with Jesus.

The more you #PrayRead the Scriptures, the more you'll enjoy the following benefits:

✦ #PrayReading is a boredom killer, making your time in the secret place more energized and engaged.

✦ Bible reading becomes relational--an interactive conversation with Jesus.

✦ You'll never run out of things to say because the Scriptures provide endless possibilities for prayer.

✦ You will pray with increased authority.

✦ Your prayers will accord with God's will.

✦ Your understanding into God's word will open.

✦ Your whole heart will align with truth and righteousness.

As you step out now from your place of prayer, would you want to take your Bible with you and pray from another Scripture as you hit the road?

✐ NOTES

Day 11
PSALMS

Reminder: We used one of Paul's prayers as our springboard yesterday to practice how to #PrayRead the Scriptures. Let's continue to work the same muscle today, this time praying in our reading from Psalms.

You've made it halfway through this Reset—fabulous! Let's renew our commitment and go the whole 20 days!

Millions of believers have a practice of praying daily from the book of Psalms—because it's so deeply meaningful, powerfully sustaining, and incredibly helpful. Hopefully you'll get hooked, too.

The book of Psalms is the Bible's songbook and prayerbook. It provides an inexhaustible treasure trove for believers who delight to sing and pray from Scripture.

The psalms David wrote were called, "The prayers

of David" (Ps 72:20). When you're meditating in a psalm, you're bathing your soul in a Spirit-inspired prayer. Listen carefully: Your prayer life will be complete only as it includes consistent engagement with the book of Psalms.

Personally, Psalms is the first Bible book I open daily. I #PrayRead there daily. My pace is relaxed because I'm not trying to break any speed records. Some psalms are finished in a day; others take several days to traverse. The end result is that I typically complete all 150 psalms around once a year.

No matter if it takes you three months or three years to get all the way through, just bask in the journey.

For today, let's #PrayRead the first part of Psalm 1.

> *Blessed is the man who walks not in the counsel of the ungodly, nor stands in the path of sinners, nor sits in the seat of the scornful. (Ps 1:1)*

PRAY the three phrases of this verse.

✦ Express to God your commitment to renounce the values and advice of ungodly people.

✦ Tell the Lord you don't want to stand or hang out in a place where sinners do their thing. Ask for wisdom to remove yourself from such places.

✦ Ask Him to save you from scoffing, with the scornful, at things that are holy or precious. Refuse a cynical spirit.

> *But his delight is in the law of the LORD, and in His law he meditates day and night. (Ps 1:2)*

PRAY the two phrases of this verse.

✦ Tell the Lord how much you delight in His word. Far from being a burden, His commands are a delight to you.

✦ Ask the Lord to expand your prayer life until you are meditating in His word day and night. Express how eagerly you long for this attainment. Entreat Him to increase your appetite for His word.

> *He shall be like a tree planted by the rivers of water, that brings forth its fruit in its season, whose leaf also shall not wither; and whatever he does shall prosper. (Ps 1:3)*

PRAY the four phrases of this verse.

✦ Since He's planted you by the river of the Spirit, draw upon His life-giving power right now.

✦ Ask Him to make you a fruitful believer. Believe for seasons of particular fruitfulness.

✦ A withered leaf speaks of drought. Even when weathering dry times, ask for a connection to His Spirit that always keeps you renewed and vibrant.

✦ As you devote yourself to righteousness, ask Him to prosper you in every way—spiritually, financially, mentally, emotionally, physically, and relationally. Apprehend the verse as a personal promise and hold to it in faith. ⏻

If you still have time, continue to pray in this manner through each verse in Psalm 1.

Now I invite you to write out the verse in Psalm 1 (or any psalm) that is meaning the most to you today:

As you hit the road, take this verse with you and #PrayRead it back to God. Want to send out a #PrayerReset post? Have a good one!

🖊 NOTES

Day 12
LISTEN

Reminder: The last couple days we prayed from Scripture while reading. The more we exercise that #PrayRead muscle, the more understanding we'll gain and the more meaningful our time with God will be.

The Lord showed me on one occasion what I believe to be the most important word in the Bible. One word of Christ's kept striking me because of how frequently He repeated it. You'll see it in these verses.

"What you hear in the ear, preach on the housetops." (Matt 10:27)

"He who has ears to hear, let him hear!" (Matt 11:15)

"Having eyes, do you not see? And having ears, do you not hear?" (Mark 8:18)

Hear. There it was. Over and over. It was the primary word in His blockbuster parable of the sower

(Matt 13). That parable revealed that the way we *hear* the word determines the fruit it produces in our lives.

Everything in the kingdom of God is predicated upon hearing. Once we hear from heaven, kingdom doors swing. Everything changes when we hear from God and act upon His word.

This is why, when we come to the secret place, we come primarily to listen. Yes, it's a time to talk to God; but more than that, it's a time to hear from God.

Things don't change when I talk to God; things change when God talks to me. When I speak, nothing happens. When God speaks, universes come into existence. In our prayer lives, therefore, we should be slow to speak and quick to listen.

I can't tell God what to say, or when to say it. But I can position myself so that, when He does speak, I'm ready to hear and respond.

We spend time in the word so we can hear from God. Someone might say, "But I never hear from God." If that's true, I will tell you why. You're not living in His word. There, I said it.

PRAY. Tell the Lord you're receiving this exhortation. Express your eagerness to hear His voice. ⏻

We see the importance of hearing in Psalm 95.

> *Today, if you will hear His voice: "Do not harden your hearts, as in the rebellion, as in the day of trial in the wilderness." (Ps 95:7-8)*

Because of hard hearts, the Israelites didn't believe and obey God. How important is this verse? Well, the writer of Hebrews quoted it six times. It's a good verse to talk to God about.

PRAY. Implore God for a soft heart—a heart that responds in faith and obedience every time He speaks. Ask for grace to learn from the example of the hard-hearted Israelites in the wilderness. *Jesus, I say yes to every word of Your mouth.* ⏻

Paul made the oft-quoted statement that *faith comes by hearing* (Rom 10:17). Faith hears. That's what Paul reinforced in this verse:

> *Therefore He who supplies the Spirit to you and works miracles among you, does He do it by the works of the law, or by the hearing of faith? (Gal 3:5)*

Take a few moments to ponder the implications of that verse.

- ✦ When faith hears the word, the supply of the Spirit is released to us.
- ✦ When faith hears the word, miracles are worked among us.

PRAY. Ask the Lord for faith that truly hears His voice and releases the life of God to others. ⏻

We want to cultivate the discipline of listening

while reading the word. We don't read so we can say, "I've completed my daily quota of Bible reading." We read in order to *hear*.

Hearing from God often happens through the most simple means:

✦ Place God's word before you.

✦ Talk to God internally as you read, turning your reading time into an interactive visit.

✦ Take time to ponder any verse the Spirit highlights to you. Ask questions about it. As you ask what the verse is saying, also ask what the verse *isn't* saying. Do other Scriptures come to mind that put a unique light on this verse?

As you take time to press into the crevices of a Scripture, you're positioned to hear from God.

Close out your reset time today by expressing how eager you are to hear His voice. Whisper your affection to Jesus.

✏ NOTES

Day 13
JOURNAL

As you #PrayRead the word, the Holy Spirit will sometimes open a Scripture to your understanding. Those insights are incredibly valuable, worth writing down. It's called *journaling.* Evidence suggests that Paul journaled:

Bring the cloak that I left with Carpus at Troas when you come—and the books, especially the parchments. (2 Tim. 4:13)

In Paul's day, *parchments* were the equivalent of today's paper notepads. It seems that Paul, while reading Scripture, scribbled his Spirit-inspired insights onto pieces of parchment. Those meditations were so precious to him that, when asking Timothy to bring his belongings, he emphasized his longing to be reunited with his journal—his collection of parchments.

The devout of all ages have journaled. The psalmist was determined to never forget the Lord's precepts (Ps 119:93). Journaling probably helped him. Write out Psalm 119:93 here:

PRAY. Talk to the Lord about this verse. Tell Him you share the psalmist's resolve. ⏻

I maintain a journal of biblical insights because of a principle taught by Jesus.

> *"Therefore take heed how you hear. For whoever has, to him more will be given." (Luke 8:18)*

The emphatic word is *how*. How should we hear? In a way that enables us to hold onto what we've received. Jesus said "more will be given" to those who retain what's been given. If we make the word He's spoken to us a permanent part of our history with Him, He'll give more.

Personally, I have a lousy memory. If I don't write

down the insights God gives me, I forget them. So I write them down and review them later. Above all, I want to retain the things God gives me. Why? Because *I want more.*

I see in football an analogy of Jesus' meaning. Suppose a wide receiver catches a football but then drops it. The quarterback winces. If the receiver drops a second pass, the quarterback is dismayed. If the receiver drops a third ball, the quarterback won't throw him any more balls. Here's the principle: To be thrown the ball, a receiver must have a reliable track record of catching and keeping footballs.

The same is true in the kingdom. If we want God to keep speaking to us from His word, we must retain what He gives. That's where a journal comes in. It's a way of retaining those things God speaks from His word *so that we might receive more.*

What's a practical way to do this? When you read a verse that suddenly means something special to you, write down both the verse and the insight received. When convenient, enter those notes into your computer or paper journal. Include the date and full text of the verse.

Then, develop a system of reviewing your entries—because retention requires review. Retention is a rigorous exercise, but we do it for one simple reason: *We want more.* And we know He gives more when we've made the effort to retain what we've already received. ⏻

PRAY. Ask for help to develop a way of retaining everything He gives you in His word. Tell Him how eagerly you want more.

Decide today how you're going to journal the insights God gives you. It will take time to perfect your system, but at least start. To begin, write your answers to these questions:

1. What style notepad will I bring to my prayer time?

---

2. Will my permanent journal be on paper or in a computer text file?

---

3. What are practical ways I can review my journal so that I never forget the things God has spoken to me?

Although it takes labor, journaling is a strategic building block that, when put in place, will help you develop a strong and consistent prayer life. You're setting yourself up for *more*.

Have a wonderful day in Christ!

✐ NOTES

Day 14
OBEY

Reminder: Jot down everything God shows you in the secret place and place it in a journal for periodic review. Why is this important? Because when we retain what God gives, He gives more.

Today's focus is on obedience. Let's start with this massive question from our Master:

"But why do you call Me 'Lord, Lord,' and not do the things which I say?" (Luke 6:46)

PRAY. Take a few moments to tremble before the weight of that question. Whisper, *You are my Lord.*

Discipleship means obedience—implicit, immediate obedience. Disciples of Christ are eager to obey every word of His mouth. We don't vet the word to determine its feasibility. We just say *yes* to the King. "Sell all." *Yes, Lord.*

Obedience isn't "the down side" or "obligatory side" of the Christian life. Actually, it's the liberating side of our faith. It makes our journey with Him joyful, bright, and life-giving. ⏻

> *But be doers of the word, and not hearers only, deceiving yourselves. (James 1:22)*

We said earlier that everything in the kingdom is predicated upon hearing, but hearing finds its fulfillment in doing. Faith acts. James said that if we don't obey we deceive ourselves.

A prayer life that hears and speaks but doesn't do is dull and lifeless. Joyful Christian living is discovered only in the meadows of obedience.

When we do what we hear in the secret place, life becomes a romantic adventure with our beloved Bridegroom. ⏻

Psalm 118 gives fantastic imagery to the glory of obedience:

> *God is the LORD, and He has given us light; bind the sacrifice with cords to the horns of the altar. (Ps 118:27)*

In this verse, the psalmist likened our surrender to the way a sacrificial bull would be bound to the altar as an offering to God. Here's why. When God gives a command, it comes with light and understanding. In joyful response, we offer our heart in total obedience, binding our soul strenuously to the altar of consecration. The verse depicts eager submission to God's will because we've seen the wisdom of His command.

Without understanding and light, the way of obedience can sometimes appear hard or harmful. But when light and understanding illumine our hearts, we realize that obedience is our safest refuge. When Jesus calls, we're safer out in the storm with Him than in the boat without Him (Matt 14:25-32).

When God calls you to do something you can't do, you're being drawn into an adventure. Get out of the boat and step onto the water. Unreserved obedience always trumps self-protective disobedience.

Has God ever called you to do something that didn't make sense? Did it appear that obedience would lead to ruin? When you chose obedience, were you surprised at how the path opened before you?

Prayer without obedience is boring. Who wants it? Therefore, since you've decided to reset your prayer life, reset your resolve to obey, too.

Is there any area of life in which you've struggled to obey Christ? If so, write it candidly here:

PRAY.

✦ Ask for His measureless love to melt from your heart any pocket of resistance to His marvelous will.

✦ Express your confidence in His leadership in your life.

✦ Tell Him that you know His command is ever-lasting life (John 12:50).

✦ Express your resolve to obey Him even unto death.

✦ Ask Him to make obedience a firm stone in your foundation so that your prayer life might be unshakable.

Obedience will make today delightful!

✎ NOTES

Day 15
LOVE

Reminder: Yesterday we renewed our resolve to obey. We follow our Savior's every word because we know obedience turns prayer into an exhilarating adventure.

Prayer is all about love. Reduce prayer to its fundamental essence and you're left with love. A prayer Reset is a return to our first love (Rev 2:4).

Scripture describes Jesus as our heavenly Bridegroom and us as His bride. It's love language, and it's expressed beautifully in Psalm 45.

Listen, O daughter, consider and incline your ear; forget your own people also, and your father's house; so the King will greatly desire your beauty; because He is your Lord, worship Him. (Ps 45:10-11)

Clearly, the love that flows between the King and His bride is *romantic*. The unique quality that distinguishes romantic love from other kinds of love is the element of *desire*. In romance, there's strong desire to be together. We just can't seem to get enough of each other.

PRAY. Express your desire for your Bridegroom, the Lord Jesus. Tell Him how much you want to be with Him and see Him. Beg for Him to return. Let love flow. His Spirit is empowering you to love Him back with the same God-sized affections with which He loves you, because it takes God to love God.

The secret place is a womb. It's where love is nurtured and grown. Yes, love is grown. When it comes to love nobody is an expert—we all need to grow in our capacity to receive and express His love. We're always searching for ways to give more of our hearts. Just as fire is never satisfied (Prov 30:16), the fiery passions of divine love are always looking for greater abandonment. More love, always more. ⏻

See how Jesus described the love we share:

> *"As the Father loved Me, I also have loved you; abide in My love… This is My commandment, that you love one another as I have loved you." (John 15:9, 12)*

Jesus said He loves us as the Father loves Him. What an amazing love that must be! Then He said that we are to love one another with that very same love.

So the love that flows between the Father and Son is the model for the love that flows between us and Christ, and then between us and others.

We thought it was enough to love our neighbor as ourselves (Matt 19:19), but Jesus raised the bar. He said we are to love our neighbor in the same way the Father loves the Son.

How can we love like this? Only by coming to the womb of the secret place and receiving His power to love.

PRAY. Launch on a quest to explore what He meant by, "Abide in My love." (John 15:9) ⏻

Consider the amazing love described in Romans:

> *For I am persuaded that neither death nor life, nor angels nor principalities nor powers, nor things present nor things to come, nor height nor depth, nor any other created thing, shall be able to separate us from the love of God which is in Christ Jesus our Lord. I tell the truth in Christ, I am not lying... For I could wish that I myself were accursed from Christ for my brethren, my countrymen according to the flesh. (Rom 8:38-9:3)*

Paul ended Romans 8 by describing the "Mount Everest" of all loves—the love of God from which *nothing* can separate us.

Then, in the verses that immediately follow (the chapter break is an artificial separation), Paul described what the highest love for our fellow man looks like. He had such a godly love for his fellow Jews that he was willing to lay down not simply his *earthly* life but his *eternal* life for them. He could wish that he were eternally accursed and separated from Christ if it could mean the salvation of his fellow Jews whom he loved.

The Romans 8 love of God had given him Romans 9 love for his fellow countrymen.

PRAY! Oh Lord, fill me with this love. Give me the heights of Romans 8 love. May this love so fill my heart that I might gain Romans 9 love for my fellow countrymen. Give me this love! ⏻

May your prayer life always rest steadfastly on a foundation of love.

As you leave your secret place, seek to nurture this flame of love all day long. Do it all for love!

✏ NOTES

Day 16
FAST

Reminder: Yesterday was all about love. We're returning to our first love. The bottom line on this Reset is the fanning of our affections for the Lord Jesus and people everywhere.

Today let's look at the gracious gift of fasting. Jesus has given it to us for at least two leading reasons: It enables us to intensify our pursuit of righteousness, and it sensitizes our hearts to receive more from God.

Jesus taught that fasting is a secret part of our prayer life.

"But you, when you fast, anoint your head and wash your face, so that you do not appear to men to be fasting, but to your Father who is in the secret place; and your Father who sees in secret will reward you openly." (Matt 6:17-18)

Jesus said, *When you fast.* He seemed to assume it would happen, which means it's normative to a disciple's prayer life.

He emphasized that He wants us to practice fasting in secret. We don't do it to show others how devout we are, but to express to Jesus how we desire Him. It's for His eyes only. ⏻

Fasting is not easy. It's tough on the appetite, the body, and the soul. It requires holy courage. So let me encourage you by showing the vital role fasting played in the life of a man named Cornelius.

> So Cornelius said, "Four days ago I was fasting until this hour; and at the ninth hour I prayed in my house, and behold, a man stood before me in bright clothing." (Acts 10:30)

Cornelius was a Roman army captain and a Gentile (that is, not a Jew). God chose his household to become the first Gentile Christians. Through Cornelius, the door of the gospel opened to the entire world. (The story is in Acts 10—it's a fascinating read.)

Why did God choose Cornelius to trigger the global spread of the gospel? We seem to find the answer in these four qualities of his life: He feared God (Acts 10:2), he prayed (Acts 10:2), he fasted (Acts 10:30), and he gave alms to the poor (Acts 10:2). God exported the piety represented by those four qualities to every nation on earth.

Fasting helped position Cornelius to be a player in a historic transition heaven was bringing to earth—the inclusion of the Gentiles in the family of God.

PRAY: Ask the Lord to reproduce in you these same four qualities: godly fear, prayer, fasting, and almsgiving. ⏻

David wrote about fasting:

> *I humbled myself with fasting. (Ps 35:13)*

Fasting is a biblical way to humble ourselves. We fast because we believe His promise that He releases more grace to the humble (1 Pet 5:5). ⏻

There are many "soft" ways to fast—such as fasting social media or sugar. But even though it's "hard," consider a water fast (or as close to a water fast as your doctor will approve). *Go for it.*

Feel free to inch your way forward. Perhaps begin by fasting dinner, and then next time do more. Want a suggestion? Try something like this:

+ Fast for 24 hours.
+ If possible, do water only (consult your doctor).
+ Plan it for a day when your schedule will allow more time for prayer.

PRAY. Do you want to plan a fast? Then write down the answers the Lord seems to give to the following questions:

1. For how long shall I plan to fast? _____
2. What kind of fast will it be? Water only? Juice only? What else shall I fast, such as media, etc.?

   _____

3. What date will the fast happen? _____
4. From what responsibilities can I free myself that day so I can devote myself more fully to prayer?

   _____

5. Will I spend part of the day in solitude? _____
6. Do I want to invite anyone to join me? If so, who?

   _____

7. What am I asking of God as I step into this fast?

   _____

   _____

After it's over, journal your experiences. What worked well for you, and what will you change next time? What was your strongest benefit? ⏻

As you go now, ask Him for grace to fast.

✎ **NOTES**

_____

_____

_____

_____

_____

Day 17
LIST

Let's talk about using a *prayer list*, which is a self-crafted list of things we aim to pray for each day.

Some believers find more traction in their prayer life when they use a prayer list. Why? Because it can provide focus, make your prayer time more productive, and help you identify answered prayer. When you see how God is answering, your confidence in prayer skyrockets.

During the next few months, I recommend you use a prayer list to help jump start your prayer life. Test drive it for a year and see if it's for you.

A list is not constricting but empowering. It helps to prime our prayer pump, so to speak, especially when our mind is foggy or scattered. We don't serve the list as though we're obligated to finish it every day; rather, the list serves us as a tool to make our prayer time more effectual. We're always free to deviate from it as our heart desires. ⏻

Prayer has many expressions, as Paul indicated:

> *Praying always with all prayer and supplication in the Spirit, being watchful to this end with all perseverance and supplication for all the saints. (Eph 6:18)*

The idea behind *all prayer* is *all kinds of prayer*. There are many ways to pray, including supplication (petition), thanksgiving, praise, intercession, adoration, meditation, etc. A well-designed prayer list will provide for all kinds of prayer. ⏻

Would you like to create your own prayer request list right now? If so, grab your notepad and let me offer some suggestions.

You may want to title this something like, *My Request List.* Divide it into three categories: Personal, People, and Circumstances.

✦ **Personal:** Jesus prayed for Himself (John 17:1-5), and so may you. Itemize the specific ways you want to pray for yourself. For example, your list might include some of the following elements: your spiritual health, physical health, soul, mind, career, finances, life purpose, ministry function, family role, etc.

✦ **People:** Pray for individuals by name or title. First, consider listing several categories of people such as family, friends, church leaders, government officials, police, military personnel, prisoners, the sick, the poor, missionaries, etc. Second, consider having three people on your list (on a rotating basis) whom you aim to name daily before the Lord.

✦ **Circumstances:** Pray for situations that need the Lord's intervention. List the various kinds of circumstances you want to keep on your radar, such as your city, Jerusalem, nations, churches, ministries, denominations, news headlines, orphans, wars, terrorism, persecuted believers, human trafficking, racism, etc.

Always take your list to your secret place. Print or write it in a way that is easy to carry, use, and update. Expect to be regularly adding and removing specific names and needs.[1]

One way to pray through your list might be to pray a "verse of the day" over every item. For example, the following verse would work well for that:

1 For more practical tips on using a prayer list, I recommend Mike Bickle's book, *Growing In Prayer*.

> *That you may walk worthy of the Lord, fully pleasing Him,*
> *being fruitful in every good work and increasing in the knowl-*
> *edge of God. (Col 1:10)*

Let's choose to pray from the phrase being *fruitful in every good work*. Start with yourself, and ask the Lord to make you *fruitful in every good work*. Then, go to your People category and pray the same phrase over everyone in that category. Finally, progress to your Circumstances category, and ask regarding every need listed there that those involved be *fruitful in every good work*.

To be *fruitful in every good work*—what a wonderful thing to ask regarding every person on your list! And that's just one phrase from one verse. Tomorrow you could pray *that you may walk worthy of the Lord* over everyone on your list. ⏻

PRAY. Let's ask the Lord for at least one answered prayer before this 20-day Reset is over.

Have a marvelous day in our Lord Jesus!

✏ **NOTES**

Day 18
ROUTINE

Reminder: Yesterday we talked about a prayer list. Did you make one? If so, grab it and use it today.

When constructing a house, a builder first of all erects a frame on the foundation. The frame supports everything that's hung on it—such as sheetrock, windows, doors, etc.

In a similar way, when building a prayer life, you need a frame upon which everything hangs. We're calling that frame *routine*. To be consistent, prayer must be founded on the rock of routine. A *prayer routine* is a clear format or sequence of steps that puts order and stability into your secret place.

Some people try to build their prayer life on the sands of inspiration. Inspiration is helpful for a moment, but it doesn't produce longevity in prayer. Routine does. Routine is deliberate not dull. It's intentional not boring.

There are many kinds of valid prayer routines. For example, some people build their prayer routine on the *Our Father* prayer Jesus gave us (Matt 6:9-13). They use each phrase as focus for a segment of their prayer time. Something like this:

✦ "Our Father in heaven, hallowed be Your name" (v.9). Prayer starts with a time of worship, thanksgiving, and praise, and is Father-centered.

✦ "Your kingdom come" (v.10). We call on Jesus to establish His kingdom in our midst. Where Jesus is King, things are done His way by His power. We can ask for His kingdom to come to every need on our request list.

✦ "Your will be done on earth as it is in heaven" (v.10). We ask for God's perfect will to be done here on earth—for Personal needs, People needs, and Circumstances on our list.

✦ "Give us this day our daily bread" (v.11). This is first of all a request for daily necessities such as food, clothing, and shelter. But we also ask Him to feed us spiritually with today's portion of bread from His word.

✦ "And forgive us our debts, as we forgive our debtors" (v.12). We labor for reconciliation in all our relationships.

✦ "And do not lead us into temptation, but deliver us from the evil one" (v.13). This is a prayer

of humility, acknowledging that we are depen-
dent on Him to deliver us from the tempter.
Walking victoriously over sin is our portion.

✦ "For Yours is the kingdom and the power and
the glory forever. Amen" (v.13). We conclude
with worship.

PRAY. Take a minute with each phrase in the
Lord's Prayer. Would you like to make the skeleton of
this prayer your daily routine? ⏻

Personally, I build my secret place routine around
what I call *simultaneous reading of Scripture*. I prefer to
#PrayRead daily in four different places of Scripture:
Psalms, the Old Testament, the Gospels, and the
Epistles. I pace each reading in order to finish the entire Bible annually. Almost everything on my prayer list
is incorporated into my language of prayer while reading and meditating in the Scriptures. For more detail
on how I structure my routine, see chapter 20 in my
book, *Secrets of the Secret Place.*

If you get dislodged from your routine, just hit the
Reset button and get back in.

To see some suggested Bible reading plans, do an
internet search or visit:

www.oasishouse.com/pages/plan.

At first your prayer routine might feel bumpy. But
as you stick with it, it'll get refined with time and you'll

develop your own cadence of walking and talking with Jesus. So let's just get started.

Consider building any or all of these elements into your prayer routine: Repentance. Cleansing. Thanksgiving. Praise. Scripture Reading. The Lord's Prayer. My Request List (from Day 17). Worship.

PRAY. Pray over the above elements. Which will you include? Write your routine here in the general order you hope to follow:

1. _____
2. _____
3. _____
4. _____
5. _____
6. _____
7. _____
8. _____

Keep this written routine before you and tweak it until the sequence feels right and becomes intuitive. I assure you that holding to a routine will help build consistency and permanence into your prayer life.

Rejoice in the Lord today!

✎ NOTES

_____

_____

_____

Day 19
ENDURE

Reminder: Write a copy of the prayer routine you constructed yesterday, and build your prayer life upon it. Can you start to follow it today?

As we approach the culmination of this 20-day prayer Reset, I want to highlight the crucial role of *endurance* in prayer. Endurance is essential if we are to approach the glorious reality Paul described of praying without ceasing (1 Thess 5:17).

It can be tempting to view this Reset as an experiment or test run, as though to say, "If I get something meaningful out of these 20 days, then I'll continue." But that's like planting a kernel of corn and saying, "If I get a harvest of corn in the next 20 days, I'll plant more."

It can be days or weeks before we begin to reap benefits from the seeds we sown in prayer. But let God's word fuel your expectation—if you'll sow you'll most certainly reap:

> *Those who sow in tears shall reap in joy. He who continually goes forth weeping, bearing seed for sowing, shall doubtless come again with rejoicing, bringing his sheaves with him. (Ps 126:5-6)*

PRAY. Ask the Lord for enduring grace to sow time, energy, and faith into your secret prayer life. ⏻

The assurance that reaping follows sowing is found in many places in Scripture. Here's one of my favorites:

> *For he who sows to his flesh will of the flesh reap corruption, but he who sows to the Spirit will of the Spirit reap everlasting life. (Gal 6:8)*

We're assured that when we sow to the Spirit we'll reap to the Spirit. As we sow to the secret place we'll eventually reap to the secret place. It's impossible to keep sowing to the Spirit without ultimately reaping authentic spiritual vitality. Let me say the same thing a couple different ways.

✦ Sow time into word meditation and you'll reap word illumination.

✦ Sow grace-empowered effort into your prayer life and you'll reap the satisfaction of a vibrant prayer life.

Endurance is key. Enduring daily in prayer is the only way a prayer life is established. This 20-day Reset is meant to help you discover that, through Christ's strength, you can do this! ⏻

Consider this powerful word from Christ:

> *"By your patience possess your souls." (Luke 21:19)*

Patience here means *endurance*. Endurance is the means by which we gain a firm grip on our eternal destiny with God.

Sheer willpower or inspiration might carry our devotional life for 20 days, but only Spirit-empowered endurance will carry us long-term.

PRAY. Call out for grace and power to endure in prayer. Let it come from the depths of your soul.

Take time to listen. Is the Holy Spirit leading you to continue in daily prayer after this Reset? Do you want to extend the promise you made on Day Two of this reset?

If so, you're invited to indicate your promise here.

My Enduring Promise to God

I hereby resolve, by God's grace, to spend at least 20 minutes a day in the secret place with Jesus, for the next _____. (Fill in the amount of time you want to commit, such as six months or three years or whatever time period you desire.)

Signature _____

Date _____

May the Lord honor your sowing with a great spiritual harvest. May His affections ravish and satisfy your soul continually. By His grace, may you discover realms of intimacy with Jesus that only enduring prayer can access.

You're going to have a blessed day abiding in His love!

✎ NOTES

Day 20
GROW

Reminder: This is a marathon, not a sprint. The Holy Spirit is eager to help you endure all the way to the end. You have grace for the race!

Today marks the fulfillment of your 20/20 resolve to pray 20 minutes a day for 20 days. Marvelous! The hardest part—starting—is behind you. Before you is the glorious adventure of growing in Christ all your days.

During this Reset, you reviewed the foundation stones upon which a prayer life is built. What was the most meaningful moment for you in these 20 days? Write it down here as a memorial.

_____

_____

What victory did you experience during these days that gives you the confidence the Lord will continue to lead you forward in triumph? Write it as a reminder to yourself.

We want to grow in Christ. We all start off as spiritual infants but no one wants to stay that way. Healthy babies keep growing. Our resolve to grow in prayer is sobered by this warning from Jesus:

> *"And because lawlessness will abound, the love of many will grow cold." (Matt 24:12)*

We live in the day of which Jesus spoke. The world is forsaking the law of God and as a consequence the devotion *of many* is growing cold.

PRAY. Call on the name of the Lord. Express your longing for spiritual health. Ask Him to enable your love for Christ to grow more and more fervent in this evil generation. ⏻

Peter turned Jesus' warning into a positive exhortation:

> *But grow in the grace and knowledge of our Lord and Savior Jesus Christ. (2 Pet 3:18)*

PRAY. *Lord, how can I keep growing in the grace and knowledge of Christ?* ⏻

Take a few moments to meditate in the following verse, and believe the promise expressed here:

> *The righteous shall flourish like a palm tree, he shall grow like a cedar in Lebanon. (Ps 92:12)*

Trees grow slowly and steadily all their days. May this grace to grow be yours!

When it comes to your prayer life, ask the Lord to help you grow in at least three ways:

- ✦ Grow in the love of Christ. This Reset isn't about discipline, determination, and checking off boxes; it's about growing in fervent love for the crucified Savior. We want a softened heart that moves with tender affection when we gaze on His glory in the word. It's all about longing and desire. This is why we pray!

- ✦ Grow in #PrayReading the Scriptures, and in the breadth of your word immersion. Do you want to get to the place where you're reading through the Bible annually?

- ✦ Grow in the amount of time you devote daily to your secret place. The point may come when 20 minutes a day will no longer satisfy.

Do you want prayer to infuse all of life? Then I suggest offering 20-second prayers randomly and spontaneously throughout each day. While you're driving or walking, for example, a 20-second conversation with Jesus can cause your affection for Him to brim all over again. 20-second visits with your Beloved throughout the day will increase your awareness of His presence.

You might ask, *Bob, can you recommend any resources to help me grow more in prayer*? Yes. For your next step, I suggest reading *Secrets of the Secret Place*. I wrote it precisely for where you're at right now, and it has a track record of helping many people. If you read it prayerfully, it will put fresh fire on the altar of your heart and fuel your desire to pray more.

You have launched into the glorious adventure of an intimate, communing relationship with Jesus Christ. May the word of Christ dwell in you richly, and may you abound in every good work!

✐ NOTES

Resources for growing in prayer:
  ✦ *Secrets of the Secret Place*, by Bob Sorge.
  ✦ *Growing in Prayer*, by Mike Bickle.
  ✦ Stay connected at PrayerReset.com

RESET DAILY CHECKLIST REMINDER

(tear-out bookmark)

+ Withdraw to the same place at the same time.

+ Declare war on every distraction.

+ Repent and be cleansed by Jesus' blood.

+ Offer thanksgiving and praise with sincere love.

+ #PrayRead the Scriptures. Follow a reading plan.

+ Listen, journal, and obey.

+ Fast occasionally.

+ Follow a prayer routine and use a request list.

+ Endure. Fulfill my prayer promise. Keep growing.

RESET 20-DAY SUMMARY

Desire: Jesus is motivating you with a strong desire to pray.

Decide: You've decided to devote 20 minutes a day, for the next 20 days, to prayer.

Reach: Refuse to allow any past failure to derail you. Get back in there and reach forward.

Fight: Demonize every distraction to prayer. This is war!

Place: Withdraw to the same place every day for prayer.

Clock: Keep to the time of day when you're at your best.

Repent: Repent as needed.

Cleanse: Be washed with Christ's blood and enter with confidence into your Father's arms.

Thanks: Make thanksgiving and praise your opener.

#PrayRead: Pray the Scriptures as you read them.

Psalms: Find vocabulary for prayer in the Psalms.

Listen: Yes, talk; but even better, listen.

Journal: Record and review everything noteworthy that comes to mind.

Obey: Resolve to obey every word He speaks through Scripture.

Love: Tell Him, over and over, that you're doing it all for love.

Fast: Fast occasionally.

List: Use a prayer request list for a year to see if it helps you.

Routine: Arrange the elements of your prayer routine into a set order and follow that format daily.

Endure: Always keep sowing to the secret place, even when not inspired, knowing you'll eventually reap a harvest.

Grow: Receive grace to keep growing in prayer all your days. There's more!

GROUP DISCUSSION QUESTIONS

Groups working through this book together can meet as often as they desire. Here are some optional questions to text or talk around.

Day 1

+ Why did you sign up for this prayer Reset?
+ What is the "one thing" you desire of Christ more than anything else?

Day 2

+ Do you feel like this Reset is a trial run, or have you made a firm decision to go the distance?
+ What stands out to you most in Luke 10:42?

Day 3

+ What does the reaching forward principle of Philippians 3:13-14 mean personally to you?
+ Are there failures from the past that you're hitting delete on? Explain.

Day 4

- ✦ What is your biggest distraction to prayer?
- ✦ Has God given you a strategy to war against that distraction?

Day 5

- ✦ Are you able to pray each day in the same place? Tell the group where prayer happens best for you.
- ✦ Do you find it easy or hard to withdraw and get quiet before God?

Day 6

- ✦ What time of day are you at your best or most alert?
- ✦ How will you adjust your schedule so you can pray around that time of day?

Day 7

- ✦ Do you struggle to confess and repent, or does it come easy?
- ✦ What have you learned about repentance that might help someone else in the group?

Day 8

- ✦ What questions do you have about the blood of Jesus that you would like answered?
- ✦ Do you intend to receive the sprinkling of Christ's blood every day?

Day 9

- ✦ Can you tell a story when someone upset you because they were so ungrateful?
- ✦ Why do you think the Lord wants us to approach Him with thanksgiving and praise?

Day 10

+ What has it been like as you've tried to #PrayRead the Scriptures?

+ Got any questions you want to ask the group about #PrayReading?

Day 11

+ What do you enjoy most about the Psalms?

+ How do you feel about the author's suggestion to spend some time each day praying from a psalm?

Day 12

+ What do you think about the author's assertion that *hear* is the most important word in the Bible?

+ Can you share with the group any secrets to hearing God more clearly?

Day 13

+ Do you journal? Why or why not? Do you plan to start?

+ Did you have any difficulty answering the three questions at the bottom of Day 13?

Day 14

+ What does Luke 6:46 mean to you personally?

+ Do you agree with the author, that prayer without obedience is dull?

Day 15

+ When we start talking about the romantic side of the gospel—love, intimacy, desire—is it easy or hard for your heart to go there? Any comments?

✦ Jesus said, "Abide in My love." What does that mean to you?

Day 16

✦ When it comes to fasting, what have been your questions, fears, struggles, and victories?

✦ Would our group want to do a fast together?

Day 17

✦ What elements have you put into your prayer request list?

✦ What three people have you put on your prayer list, and why?

Day 18

✦ What is the skeleton of your prayer routine?

✦ Were you able to find a Bible Reading Plan you think will work well for you?

Day 19

✦ How can we endure in daily prayer when we lose inspiration and motivation?

✦ Did you sign a promise to keep enduring in prayer past this Reset? Why or why not?

Day 20

✦ How do you want to grow in prayer?

✦ Are we interested in studying another book on prayer as a group? Do we want to keep meeting?

BOB SORGE'S TITLES

Prayer:

Reset

Secrets Of The Secret Place

Secrets Of The Secret Place: Companion Study Guide
    For Personal Reflection & Group Discussion

Secrets Of The Secret Place: Leader's Manual

Unrelenting Prayer

Illegal Prayer

Power of the Blood

Minute Meditations

Worship:

Exploring Worship: A Practical Guide to Praise and
    Worship

Glory: When Heaven Invades Earth

Following The River: A Vision For Corporate Worship

Enduring Faith:

In His Face

The Fire Of Delayed Answers

The Fire Of God's Love

Pain, Perplexity, & Promotion: A Prophetic
    Interpretation of the Book of Job

Opened From the Inside: Taking the Stronghold of
    Zion

Between the Lines: God is Writing your Story

The Chastening of the Lord

(over)

Leadership:
Dealing With the Rejection and Praise of Man
Envy: The Enemy Within
Loyalty: The Reach Of The Noble Heart
It's Not Business It's Personal
A Covenant With My Eyes

Bob's books are available at:
- ✦ Oasis House, 816-767-8880
- ✦ oasishouse.com
- ✦ christianbook.com
- ✦ amazon.com
- ✦ Kindle, iBooks, Nook, Google Play, Audible.com

twitter.com/BOBSORGE
facebook.com/BobSorgeMinistry
Blog: bobsorge.com

To see Bob's films, go to youtube.com and enter a search for "Bob Sorge Channel"